6/17/2001

Happy Birthday –
love, Bethany + Brad

The Meaning of Flowers

The Meaning of Flowers

❧ MYTH, LANGUAGE & LORE ❧

By Gretchen Scoble and Ann Field

COLLAGES BY ANN FIELD

Photography by Holly Lindem

CHRONICLE BOOKS

SAN FRANCISCO

For Matt, Kyle and Nicole —GS

For Clive, my constant inspiration —AF

Library of Congress Cataloging-in-Publication Data:
Scoble, Gretchen. The meaning of flowers / by Gretchen Scoble and Ann Field;
collages by Ann Field; photography by Holly Lindem.
p. cm.
ISBN 0-8118-1931-0
1. Flower language. 2. Symbolism of flowers. I. Field, Ann. II. Title.
GR780.S4 1998
398'.368213—dc21   97-30802
                           CIP
Printed in Hong Kong.

Book and cover design by Gretchen Scoble.

Distributed in Canada by Raincoast Books
9050 Shaughnessy Street
Vancouver, British Columbia V6P 6E5

10 9 8 7

Chronicle Books LLC
85 Second Street
San Francisco, California 94105

www.chroniclebooks.com

Introduction

FLOWERS CALL TO US. They speak a language we almost hear. Each flower's color seems an announcement. The single wildflower by the path murmurs its particular name. In a vase, they sing in chorus. Our poetic relationship with flowers may arise from the function of blossoms in nature. Flowers are beautiful and odorous for a reason: to spread pollen and engender their kind. Maybe this basic association has always reminded our species of its own engendering.

We have always worn flowers in our hair. In our literature of love—east and west, north and south—we have woven flowers into myths and stories and given them meanings. We have presented them to one another, found beauty in their blooms. We have taken flowers as emblems and composed of them a language of our own.

Since ancient times, we also have invested these floral organs with magical powers, especially in the matter of love. The periwinkle's spell engendered love; the myrtle kept it alive. In a fragrant midsummer night's dream, pansies placed on the eyes of a sleeper induced passion for the one who woke him. A distant lover, blowing on a forget-me-not, could perceive the loved one's very thoughts.

Asia honored flowers with its own profound tradition. The daylily, which in England was said to indicate flirtation, in China symbolized fertility. The first flower mentioned in literature is the lotus, the flowering water lily, which in China came to symbolize perfect truth and purity and was associated with Buddha himself. In India, the Hindus said that before creation the world was a golden lotus, the Madripadma or Mother Lotus. The god Brahma was born from this golden lotus, and he is often represented seated within the calyx of the flower.

Many of the flowers now so familiar in the West—chrysanthemums, wisteria, peonies—have Asian origins. The Japanese especially have found significance in flowers. Japanese poets saw the transience of life in the morning glory and an image of prosperity in the camellia. The symbolic meanings assigned to the blooms informs the ancient Japanese art of flower arrangement. The most popular card game in Japan has suits representing the flowers of the year.

In the West, flowers have been given meanings since time immemorial. Modern feelings for flowers were articulated, perhaps most perceptively, by the Romantic poets. The Romantics praised flowers and found themselves in their blooms. In possibly his most characteristic poem, John Keats identifies with Narcissus, the legend and the flower. By a pool in the woods, he sees that forlorn blossom drooping over its own watery image, and imagines Narcissus, who drowned in self-love, gazing at his own face this way. Though Robert Herrick had written of the fleeting bloom of the daffodil ("Fair daffodils, we weep to see/You haste away so soon."), William Wordsworth made it new. Walking the vales and hills more than a century later, he comes upon a host of golden daffodils, recalling it afterward in motion like the sea.

By the end of the Romantic period, this sublimity of flowers had crystallized into a social code for Victorian ladies and gentlemen. Courtship then was nothing if not discreet. Within that context, flowers came to serve a specific purpose as a secret code. A bouquet might bear a message. The number of leaves on a decorative branch might indicate the date and time of a secret rendezvous, the blooms the emotional intent of the exchange. In no period was it more true that "sweet flowers alone can say," as Thomas Hood had written, "what passion fears revealing."

From these secret codes for flowers, the Victorian "Language of Flowers" was created. Lists circulated, providing sometimes

different meanings for each flower. The fragrant tuberose became an invitation to dangerous pleasures. A double daisy was said to mean, "I feel as you do." "The Language of Flowers" was a parlor game, as well as a way in which discreet couples might communicate. After all, they were just flowers. Queen Victoria herself—reserved in matters of sex—had sketched the blooms in the Royal Gardens at Kew. During Victoria's reign, a number of flower code books were published. Coded bouquets were, for a time, quite the rage.

So, in ways specific and poetic, sensual and implicit, the urge to name the flowers, to know them and to give them stories, has long possessed us. Even the odor of flowers seems to promise us something. "A flower's scent—invisible yet real," writes Beverly Seaton, "has long been the emblem of the human soul." This book explores some of the mythic and personal significance of flowers, drawing upon the botany, the literature, and the lore of blooms to describe each one's acquired significance. This brief compendium looks to both the East and West for its inspiration, gathering the meanings we have given to flowers as we might gather the blooms themselves.

Amaryllis

[HIPPEASTRUM]

The amaryllis, taller than other flowers, suggested pride to the Victorians in England.

Its startling hornlike blossom erupts from the stem, shooting straight up and often eclipsing the smaller flowers in the garden. This explosion of bloom is one reason that the Greeks named this flower amaryllis, *meaning splendor. One is reminded of Dylan Thomas's evocation of "the force that through the green fuse drives the flower."*

[MAGNOLIA]

The laurel-leaved garden magnolia expressed dignity to the Victorians. The wild, swamp-dwelling magnolia suggested perseverance.

The magnolia is an ancient species, millions of years older than Homo sapiens. First to cultivate magnolias were the Chinese, who loved them for their beauty, and flavored soups with their buds. In China, the magnolia is an emblem of gentleness and feminine beauty.

In the American South, the magnolia is the tree of society. Growing up to eighty feet tall and casting fragrance from its creamy white blossoms, the magnolia perfumes the cotillion in the southern night.

The magnolia's heavy pod exposes scarlet seeds in the fall.

Peony

[PAEONIA]

The peony grants its recipient the power to keep a secret. In its tightly clenched petals, nymphs could hide.

A deep-rooted plant, the peony stands firm in the earth. A horse was needed, it was said, to pull the peony from the ground. Because of this, the peony was reputed to enhance the power of a promise. For the same reason, peonies suggested bashfulness to Victorian England.

Peonies have been cultivated in Asia for more than a thousand years. Requiring such careful cultivation, they were flowers that only the rich could afford to grow in Japan. Therefore the peony symbolizes prosperity for the Japanese.

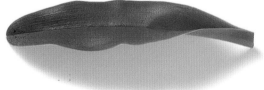

Orchid

The orchid stands for **ecstasy**.

Orchids seem to be glories from the underworld, their folds and openings, their intense scent almost too much for daylight. In the wild, they grow in the rain forests of the tropics, parasitical and peculiar, bearing beauty marks and brilliant spots, like hieroglyphics of desire.

There are over twenty-five thousand species of orchid, more than any other flower. Because of their strangeness, we have cast many names upon them: Adder's Tongue, Ram's Horn, Lady's Slipper.

Sweet Pea.

[LATHYRUS ODORATUS]

Because the sweet pea blooms constantly, the flower stood for
lasting pleasure in the Victorian language of flowers.

*Sweet peas were first imported to England from Sicily in 1699, bringing to
that northern land the casual splendor of the Mediterranean. The sweet pea's
riotous, curling tendrils and richly colored blooms also make it an emblem
of careless luxury.*

SWEET PEAS

CARD SEED CO.

Buttercup

[RANUNCULUS ACRIS]

The buttercup stands for **childishness** and ingratitude.

In the meadow, the buttercup seems to offer a quaff of love's medicine, creamy and sweet. Bright and reflective, the wild buttercup casts a radiant glow that on the skin of the neck detects a love for butter, children claim.

In ancient times, buttercups in the meadows were gathered for other uses. Buttercups could cure lunatics, it was thought in the Middle Ages. Shakespeare, who wrote of poets, lunatics, and lovers, called the buttercup the cuckoo-bud.

[ALLIUM]

The allium has been associated with great good fortune and prosperity.

Though its blossoms smell quite sweet, its stems taste like onion. Like the other members of its family—onions and garlic—allium was thought to ward off the evil eye, an invisible, unknown watcher who brought harm to human beings and cattle.

In The Odyssey, the spell of the sorceress Circe—to turn Ulysses into a pig—is warded off by an allium.

Rosemary

[ROSMARINUS OFFICINALIS]

Rosemary is for **remembrance**.

So said mad Ophelia, echoing the traditional meaning for this fragrant herb.

In England, rosemary was used in a spell to induce clairvoyant dreams. On the eve of St. Mary Magdalen, July 22, three young women, none of them yet twenty-one years old, might dip rosemary sprigs in a mixture of rum, wine, gin, vinegar, and water, then speaking no word, each drink three times, place the rosemary sprig between her breasts, and go to bed. The night would bring true dreams and a clear path for the future.

Anne of Cleves, marrying King Henry VIII, wore a crown of rosemary.

Gerbera

[GERBERA JAMESONII]

The gerbera suggests enduring purity.

Also called the Transvaal daisy, these big, bright flowers come from the hottest climates of Asia and Africa. Crowning the tops of their long stems, the blooms have perfect petals in holiday colors—white, yellow, red, orange—and in more delicate pastel shades.

Gerberas are pretty and strong. When cut, they may live three weeks in a vase with water.

Crocus

[CROCUS VERNUS]

To the Victorians, the crocus stood for youthful gladness and carried the cautionary message, "do not abuse."

Dedicated to St. Valentine, crocuses appear near his day, among the first flowers to bloom in the spring. Eager for that early pollen, the bee makes its music inside the cup of the crocus bloom.

The scent of crocuses is mysterious and alluring, said to disperse drowsiness and quicken the pulse. Cleopatra made an ointment for her hands of the subtle oil of crocuses. At the dawn of Western culture, Homer put crocuses in the marriage bed of the King and Queen of Heaven: "The flaming crocus made the mountain glow."

Forget-me-not

[MYOSOTIS]

Forget-me-nots are the **keepsake** flower, holding the beloved in memory.

A clumsy knight, the story goes, was walking by a swift river with his lady and stooped in his heavy armor to pick for her some nameless wildflowers from the bank. In due course these blooms were called forget-me-nots.

The forget-me-not is a long-lived and hardy flower, requiring just a little care to flourish.

Lily

[LILIUM]

The pure white lily in Victorian flower language translated as youthful **innocence.**

The lily is deeply identified with the ancient goddesses of the Western world. In Rome, it was said that the first lily sprang from the breast milk of the Great Goddess Juno, empress of nature. In the Middle East, the lily was sacred to Astarte, the primal goddess of fertility. Christianity too associated the lily with the feminine deity, ascribing it to the Virgin Mary.

The English word chalice *is derived from* calyx, *the cup of the lily flower.*

Chrysanthemum

[CHRYSANTHEMUM MORIFOLIUM;
DENDRANTHEMA GRANDIFLORUM]

Because the chrysanthemum blooms in November, it stands for the light of hope in dark times.

A noble flower in Asia, the chrysanthemum is mentioned by Confucius and often appears on Chinese ceramics as the flower of autumn, a symbol of harvest, rest, and ease. A Chinese painter might have spent an entire lifetime trying to render one chrysanthemum's delicate bloom. The rising sun on the Japanese flag also resembles a chrysanthemum.

In the Victorian flower code, a white chrysanthemum stood for truth, a yellow chrysanthemum for slighted love.

[DAHLIA]

The dahlia suggests the **instability** of perfect beauty.

In the gardens of the Aztecs, the conquistadors found the dahlia, a jewel of the Americas. When it was sent back to Spain, they made a holiday in its honor, the Day of the Dahlia. Some dahlias bear flowers more than a foot across.

For all its glory, the dahlia was touchy in the northern gardens and often would not survive. So the English flower code books called the dahlia fickle. In Europe, the dahlia became, nonetheless, an expensive and fashionable flower.

The tuber of the dahlia is a sweet fruit, eaten as a treat in the Americas, where the Aztecs called it cocoxochitl *(co-COX-oh-cheetle).*

Narcissus

[NARCISSUS]

In the West, the narcissus suggests egotism.

This meaning for the narcissus arises from a dark myth, that of a young man whose vanity led to the destruction of the nymph who loved him. This flower often stands sadly by a pool, nodding at its own reflection.

To the Chinese, the narcissus is the sacred lily, symbol of purity and promise.

Jasmine

[JASMINUM]

The jasmine is an emblem of good luck and increase.

When Vasco da Gama returned from his circumnavigation of the globe in the sixteenth century, he brought home a small, fragrant, white flower from the Far East. The flower's Chinese name, yeh-hsi-ming, was anglicized to jasmine.

A servant working for the legendary Medici family in Italy was said to have stolen a branch of jasmine from his master to give to his bride. By law only the duke was allowed to grow jasmine. Yet the couple grew many more plants from their single cutting, enough to sell. So Italian brides often wear a sprig of jasmine on their wedding day, hoping for increase and good luck.

Gardenia

[GARDENIA JASMINOIDES]

In the Chinese tradition, the gardenia represents feminine grace, subtlety, and artistry.

In the American South, the gardenia stands for hospitality, for the grace of the southern style of life. Its fragrant blooms perfume the streets of the French Quarter in New Orleans.

In the nineteenth century in England, the elegant gardenia was one of the few flowers considered suitable to adorn the lapel of a gentleman's formal evening jacket. Any more extravagant a bloom might have been in bad taste.

Dogwood

[CORNUS]

The dogwood stands for **endurance,** for durability through all seasons.

Though we know them mostly as shrubs, dogwoods in the wild may tower, growing to seventy-five feet. In spring, the dogwood explodes into white bloom; in summer, it offers fine, open shade and clusters of red fruit. Pioneers in the American West made sweet preserves of dogwood berries. Even at year's end, the dogwood's yellow twigs grace the winter garden.

The dogwood sends its long stems underground; from these subterranean stems, the new trees grows.

Yellow Rose

[R o s a]

In the Victorian flower language, a yellow rose spoke of
jealousy.

*In the western United States, the yellow rose spoke of love familiar, humble,
native to the land. The yellow rose is the prairie rose, the remote rose, the
extraordinary in the ordinary. It bears a beauty equal to that of other roses,
but also speaks of home, of the too-often-overlooked glories of domestic
happiness.*

*The humble yellow rose was immortalized in a popular cowboy song:
"The yellow rose of Texas is the only girl for me."*

Red Rose

When the poet Robert Burns compared his lover to a red, red rose, he was touching on the West's most ancient and potent flower lore, the identification of the red rose with beauty and with deep and passionate love.

The red rose is often identified as well with love's pain. In Greek myth, the goddess of love herself, Aphrodite, was said to have created the first red rose. Rushing to comfort her lover, Adonis—who had been gored by a wild boar— she scratched herself on the thorns. Her immortal blood forever stained the roses red.

When Cleopatra decided to seduce the Roman soldier Mark Antony, she met him in a chamber filled two feet deep with red rose petals.

White Rose

[ROSA]

The white rose suggests purity and **silence.**

White has always expressed qualities beyond the physical—love beyond the body, love of the soul. The white rose is sometimes called "the flower of light."

In Asian tradition, white stands for the ultimate absence, death. In Japan, funeral armbands are white. So the white rose may also stand for the mortal power of love, which as the Song of Songs says, is "strong as death."

Wisteria

In Asia, wisteria is an emblem of gentleness and
obedience. Similarly, for the Victorians, it said,
"I cling to thee."

*The languid and aromatic wisteria, topping the garden wall, promises a life
of luxury and ease. Wisteria bears a multitude of delicately hued flowers, pale
purple, light blue, mauve, and white. In Japan, wisteria was the flower of two
seasons, as it bloomed in April and marked the transition between spring and
summer.*

*Far at sea, sailors smelled wisteria before they saw the island on which
it grew.*

[DELPHINIUM]

Swiftness and light, says the delphinium.

The name delphinium is derived from the Greek for "dolphin," because the points and flukes of this flower's petals reminded the Greeks of the fins and nose of that graceful marine mammal. In the tall spikes of these blue and white flowers one might well imagine the leaping dolphin, quick and bright above the froth.

[ANEMONE]

The anemone suggests **abandonment.**

The goddess of love herself adored the boy Adonis, from whose blood, as he lay
dying, the scarlet anemones sprang. So the Greeks believed. In the medieval
Christian tradition, anemones were said to have grown on the hill beneath
the cross where the blood of Christ had fallen.

Known as the windflower, the anemone flourishes in high, blustery
terrain. The Greeks also spoke of it as the favorite of Zephyr, the god of the
west wind. The hue of the anemone has "a purity," D. H. Lawrence wrote,
"that suggests condensed light."

Heliotrope

[HELIOTROPIUM ARBORESCENS]

The sun-loving heliotrope suggested **devotion** to the Victorians.

These pale mauve flowers have a strong sweet scent of almonds or cherry pie. Thomas Jefferson referred to heliotrope as "a delicious flower."

One of its varieties has been known in Europe since the dawn of the West, though the variations brought from Peru in the eighteenth century stirred public amazement.

[IRIS]

The sleek and stately iris brings a **message** of hope or sorrow.

It unfolds its petals when winter still grips the earth. Perhaps because of its early bloom (sometimes arising even from the snow), the Greeks named the iris after their messenger goddess, who guided the soul to eternity after death. In ancient Egypt, the iris was deeply honored. A garland of irises even graced the Sphinx's brow.

In Japan, the iris is called ayame *and is the flower of May.*

Bachelor's Button

[CENTAUREA CYANUS]

The blue bachelor's button stands for hope in solitude.

This vivid azure flower grows well between the rows of corn, on stems so tough they were said to blunt the reaping tools, and so were also known as hurt-sickle. Its botanical name refers to the legend of Hercules and the half-man, half-horse Centaur. Shot by the poisoned arrow of Hercules, the Centaur found that these blue blossoms could heal him.

They are called bachelor's buttons from another belief, though—this one from the Middle Ages in England. A girl who placed such a bloom beneath her apron might have any bachelor she desired.

[V I O L A   W I T T R O C K I A N A]

Pansies represent the thoughts of lovers, shared before a word is spoken.

Named for the French word for "thought" (pensée), the pansy was said to be a charmed flower, possessing telepathic magic. Attending to the plucked bloom, you could hear your lover's thoughts.

Familiarly called johnny-jump-ups, pansies were widely cultivated in the nineteenth century. A perfect pansy, it was thought, had deep clear color, a circular skirt, a variegated fringe, and a single, bright, central eye.

Nasturtium

[TROPAEOLUM MAJUS]

Nasturtiums, to the Victorians, indicated a jest.

Nasturtium means "a twist of the nose." They taste peppery, like watercress.

Nasturtium plants are greedy for sunlight, and throw out dozens of round, shieldlike leaves. Beneath these shady parasols, wrinkled blossoms of scarlet and gold unfurl. Nasturtiums dangle like vines and can't seem to make up their minds whether they are flowers or food.

PARIS VIII'
TEL. ELYSÉES 84-58

Lavender

[LAVANDULA]

In Victorian times, a gift of lavender meant, I don't trust you, perhaps because the plant was sometimes used to mask a bad odor.

The lavender plant grows well in the south of France, once a Roman province. Over the millennia, the tiny flowers, the distinctive smell, and the color of lavender have filled the valleys of Provence.

In Rome itself, a sprig of lavender was often used in laundering—its name may come from the Latin "to wash"—and was often placed between the sheets. Because lavender washed lovers with its sweet perfume, it might also stand for renewal.

Heather

[CALLUNA VULGARIS]

Red heather promised **passion.** White heather offered
protection from rash, passionate acts.

*In late summer, the rosy purple cover of heather spreads over the heath and
moorland of northern England and, especially, Scotland. So northerners, come
south to find work, felt nostalgia at the thought of heather and yearned for
home.*

*Heather stuffed in a mattress makes a springy bed. Such mattresses,
shipped across the Atlantic, brought wild heather to the Americas, where
it flourishes today.*

Bees fed on heather produce a dark and tangy honey.

Lilac

[SYRINGA]

Lilacs express the **beautiful sadness** of love, the feeling—always available to the lover—of impending farewell.

Lilacs are purple and white and, as is often the case with these hues, suggest both passion and absence. In European folklore, the white lilac is said to have once been the purple, blanched overnight on the grave of a young suicide wrongly convinced that she, like Juliet, had been forsaken. In the white bloom we find her passion departed but her farewell forever.

The people of the English countryside considered lilacs the quintessential bloom of May, embodying the all-too-brief perfection of spring. For this reason, the Victorians identified lilac with the first emotion of love. Potently fragrant, the flower was once thought capable of warding off the Black Death itself.

Hydrangea

[HYDRANGEA MACROPHYLLA]

In Victorian England, to send someone hydrangeas was to suggest that he or she had been boasting.

Originally a marsh plant native to Asia, the hydrangea was introduced to Europe in the eighteenth century.

It was associated with boastfulness because it produced such magnificent flowers, but no fruit.

Aster

[ASTER]

Asters speak of the tiny **beginnings** from which all great things proceed.

Asters were said to originate when the goddess Virgo scattered some stardust on the earth. Where it fell, asters sprang up. The name aster *means star. Clusters of these small daisylike flowers with yellow centers reminded people of the night sky.*

In Europe, asters have long been supposed to have magical powers. Their watchful and beneficial "eyes" could drive away evil spirits. An ointment made

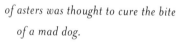

of asters was thought to cure the bite of a mad dog.

Zinnia

[ZINNIA]

The Victorian meaning of the zinnia was absence, as well as its emotional correlation, sorrow.

The conquistadors found zinnias in Mexico as they traversed the wilderness in 1519. Wild zinnias weren't much—the flowers dingy purple or muddy yellow. But in the hands of gardeners, the zinnia has undergone a startling transformation. Now it appears in many bright colors and varieties.

In 1920, the botanist Luther Burbank produced the most beautiful variety, Zinnia elegans, a stunning dahlialike flower.

Hyacinth

Young love, so transcendent, so self-obsessed, so often fatal, manifests itself in the hyacinth's blooms. In the French flower code, it said, "You love me and destroy me." In the English code, it merely suggested play.

The gods Apollo and Zephyr both loved a glorious mortal youth, Hyacinth, but Zephyr killed him when he discovered that Hyacinth preferred Apollo. From his blood grew the blossoms that bear his name. So the flower is thought of as a consolation for the lost love of youth.

The Koran praises the hyacinth. If you have just two loaves left, the book recommends, sell one and buy hyacinths, "to feed thy soul."

Hollyhock

[ALCEA ROSAEA]

Hollyhocks stand for fertility, for ease of creation and abundance.

Originally a Chinese flower, grown for the savory taste of its leaves, the hollyhock was brought to England in the sixteenth century. There the English gardeners discovered how fast the plant grew and how many seeds it produced. This culinary plant soon towers over the garden wall, showing off its stunning and various blooms.

Make love a daily habit, the hollyhock seems to say, and something grand and imposing will arise.

Honeysuckle

[LONICERA]

Because it winds its long wild stems around the branch, honey-suckle reminded the Victorians of **the bonds of love,** as if it said to the object of love, "Let me bind you—be my captive."

In the tropics, this fast-growing flowering vine can cover a fence in a week, transforming it into a fragrant, bushy wall. The honeysuckle's scent is the epitome of June. Broken from its stem, the trumpetlike petal bears a drop of sugary transparent liquid, which one may touch to the tongue.

Shakespeare called them woodbine. The honeysuckle's botanical name is caprifolium, meaning goat flower. As goats were famous as lusty creatures, perhaps this name suggests that honeysuckle has aphrodisiac properties.

Tulip

[T U L I P A]

In Persia, to give a red tulip was **to declare your love.**
The black center of the red tulip was said to represent the
lover's heart, burned to a coal by love's passion. To give a
yellow tulip was to declare your love hopelessly and utterly.

*Wild tulips are native to Persia, and first came to be known in Europe in
1559, when a traveler, astonished by the tulips he had seen in a secret garden
in Constantinople, brought some home. In Holland, the tulip was a sensation
and became so popular that bulbs fetched huge prices. Speculation in tulip
bulbs continued until the market collapsed, plunging the country's whole
economy into depression.*

The word tulip *is derived from the Turkish word for turban* (tülbent),
so-called because of the shape of its bloom.

Sunflower

[HELIANTHUS ANNUS]

The sunflower promises **power,** warmth, nourishment—
the attributes of the sun itself. In the Inca cultures of the
Andes, the sunflower was revered. The flower's image was
hammered into gold and placed in the temple.

*The sunflower's muscular turning, as it follows the sun across the sky, provides
an image of potent loyalty. The plant is also useful in every part—the seeds for
eating, the stalks for fodder, the leaves for cloth.*

*This brilliant bold flower towers over the garden. Italian sunflowers
have grown to forty feet tall. In Chinese symbolism, the sunflower represents
longevity.*

Daffodil

The daffodil stood for **chivalry** in Victorian England, perhaps because it sometimes stood in the snow, waiting for the rest of the flowers of spring.

This crisp bloom's name can be traced to the Old English **affodyle***, meaning early arrival. "The sweet o' the year," wrote Shakespeare, "when daffodils begin to peer."*

Pointing a finger at a daffodil bud was said to prevent it from blooming. Reputedly, it is unlucky to take a daffodil into a henhouse.

Marigold

[CALENDULA OFFICINALIS]

Ardent, bittersweet, true, the marigold lifts its bloom to the sun year round—its *little lover,* some call it.

In England, they were first called "golds." In the Middle Ages, they came to adorn the Virgin Mary and afterward bore her name. "Open afresh your round of starry folds," wrote Keats, "Ye ardent marigolds."

In Victorian flower language, though, the marigold referred to grief or cruelty. Its botanical name, Calendula, means "a bloom a month."

Primrose

[PRIMULA VULGARIS]

The primrose stands for youth and hope. Ointment from primrose petals has even been used as a wrinkle cream.

The primrose is especially beloved by the English. It's been written that England "carries a primrose in her heart."

In Switzerland, mountaineers as they climbed carried primroses as an antidote to vertigo.

[GLADIOLUS]

Gladioli stand for **natural grace.**

*Glads, as they are known familiarly, grew wild and abundantly in the Middle
East, and are thought to be the flowers that Jesus referred to in the Sermon
on the Mount, calling them the "lilies of the field... even Solomon in all his
glory was not arrayed like one of these."*

*One African species of gladiolus grows only in the spray where the Zambesi
River flows over Victoria Falls.*

Bird~of~Paradise

[STRELITZIA REGINAE]

The extraordinary tropical bloom of the bird-of-paradise suggests that something **strange and wonderful** is about to occur.

Native to southern Africa, this flower attracts a particular species of bird that shares its colors—orange with a touch of dark blue.

In Asia, it is also known as the crane lily for its shape, which resembles a folded paper crane.

[ACACIA]

The mimosa stands for **sensitivity**.

The feathery, furry mimosa is known for its exquisite touch. It will actually withdraw its leaves if disturbed. Its blooms are fuzzy yellow balls, yet its branches are thorny.

In India, the mimosa is said to have grown out of a falcon's claw. Demons wounded the bird as it tried to steal the elixir of the gods. Where its claw fell to earth, up sprang the mimosa, which can both soothe and prick.

In Arabia, a sprig of mimosa hung above the bed was said to lengthen love and ward off spells of jealousy.

Plumeria

[PLUMERIA RUBRA]

A tropical flower, plumeria stands for love in long absence, as for the sailor long at sea. The flower of the traditional Hawaiian lei, it will always say "Aloha."

Known as frangipani, this small tree flowers all year. The petals of its white, pink, and deep rose blooms remain fragrant for weeks after the flower is cut. In Asia, the plumeria is known as the temple tree.

Camellia

[CAMELLIA JAPONICA]

The camellia stood for **honest excellence.** It told a Victorian lover, "My destiny is in your hands."

The excellence of camellias lies in their big beautiful blooms and evergreen leaves. It "boasts no fragrance and conceals no thorn," wrote one anonymous poet of this gorgeous flower.

Now identified with the Old South, the camellia is a native of Japan.

Snapdragon

[ANTIRRHINUM MAJUS]

In the Victorian flower language, the snapdragon stood for presumption. "Let's be impetuous," this flower said.

In the garden, snapdragons jump up in unexpected places, raising their popcorn blooms above the other flowers on long sturdy stalks. The open blooms will gently bite down on an inserted finger—hence the name.

A garland of snapdragons confers pluck upon its wearer.

Ranunculus

[RANUNCULUS ASIATICUS]

This small charming flower was said in Victorian times to tell a lover that he or she was rich in charm and attraction.

The name ranunculus *means little frog in Latin, so called because the Roman naturalist Pliny found these flowers in low, damp places, among the frogs.*

There are more than 250 species of ranunculus; even the delphinium is part of the family. In Japan, one species is a climber with proliferous blooms, growing to ten feet. In southern Europe, a smaller variety bears white and sky-blue blooms. The buttercup is a wild ranunculus.

Hibiscus

[HIBISCUS ROSA-SINENSIS]

A gift of hibiscus might suggest, "Seize this opportunity."

A symbol of delicate beauty, the large blooms of the hibiscus are open for just a short period every day. Flower-of-an-hour, it has been called.

Originally from Africa, the hibiscus is beloved in the South Pacific. There a red hibiscus behind a girl's right ear meant "I have a lover." Behind her left ear, it meant "I seek a lover." Behind both: "I have a lover and *I seek a lover."*

The hibiscus is the state flower of Hawaii. Its blossoms make a rich tea.

Freesia

[F R E E S I A]

A gift of freesia reminds a loved one that love may be careful
and calm, as well as rushed and passionate.

*Freesia's neat, classical lines reminded the poet Joshua Freeman Crowell
of altars to Aphrodite, the goddess of love.*

*Originally from South Africa, this plant was once considered rather
dowdy. In the hands of horticulturalists, however, it produced myriad bright
offspring in many colors, even copper.*

[Cydonia oblonga]

Quince stands for **temptation.**

Some sources say it was a quince and not an apple that Eve ate in the Garden of Eden. The quince may also be the original "golden fruit" of the Hesperides, object of many a quest.

The tart fruit of the quince has, since Greek times, been a token of desire and fertility. Plutarch counseled young women to eat quinces in preparation for their wedding night.

The first marmalade was made in Spain, out of quinces.

Anthurium

[A N T H U R I U M]

A gift of anthurium confesses a man's intense **attraction.**

Also known as the tail flower and the flamingo flower, the anthurium manages somehow to be both comic and impressive.

The novelist J. K. Huysmans described anthurium: "There sprang from the middle of this bright, vermillion heart a fleshy, downy tail, all yellow and white." The spathe or "tail" of the anthurium is actually a spike of many tiny flowers.

Native to South America, these flowers in northern latitudes will survive only in a heated greenhouse.

Pomegranate

[PUNICA GRANATUM]

The pomegranate stands for **unspoken desire.** Inside, its scarlet pips glow like rubies.

A native of Persia, the pomegranate has an ancient relationship with humanity. It appears in the sculpture of the oldest Western civilizations. The ancient Song of Songs mentions the pomegranate. Desirous, the lover goes to the orchard, to see if "the pomegranate trees are in flower."

In the Chinese flower calendar, the pomegranate is the flower of June, a symbol of progeny and posterity. In the Victorian flower language, pomegranates indicated "foolishness."

[PROTEA]

Protea suggest that the **challenge of desire** takes many forms.

When Ulysses wrestled Proteus, the Greek god transformed himself into a lion, an elephant, a handful of water, making himself quite a formidable opponent. This large flowering plant, which bears the god's name, also exists in many forms. More than fourteen hundred species make up the Proteaceae family, some of them known familiarly as King and Queen Protea, Rose Spoon, Pink Mink, Silver Tree, and Blushing Bride.

European explorers first observed protea in South Africa in the 1600s. Now many are grown in Southern California, thriving in the heat and aridity.

Violet

[VIOLA ODORATA]

The violet is a pledge of **faithfulness.**

In his sonnets, Shakespeare used the violet as a symbol of humility and constancy in love.

As if shy, these rich dark flowers withdraw their color to the shadowy glade. "How they would lose their beauty," wrote Keats, "were they to throng into the highway crying out, 'Admire me—I am a violet.'"

A dream of violets was said to foretell an advancement in life.

Queen Anne's Lace

[DAUCUS CAROTA]

Queen Anne's lace stands for **self-reliance**.

In the rain, the stems of Queen Anne's lace bow down, to protect its pollen from the raindrops. A member of the parsley family, this plant has small creamy flowers in dense heads surrounding a single central purple blossom. The white blooms have been likened to the Queen's frilly headdress, the dark central flower to a single drop of her royal blood.

In England, it was considered bad luck to bring Queen Anne's lace indoors.

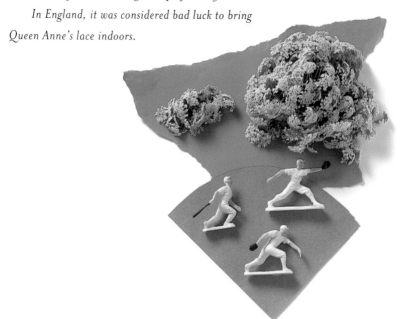

Periwinkle

[VINCA]

To know someone a long time and to know someone well, this is the promise of the periwinkle.

You have to look hard, sometimes, to see these blooms of blue and white amid the deep green clusters of periwinkle leaves. The French know the periwinkle as the virgin's flower, for its readiness and reticence. In England, periwinkles are sold with a song.

In lore, a bunch of these delicate, pastoral blooms, carried in a pocket, evoked sweet memories of a lover long gone.

Poppy

[PAPAVER]

The poppy suggests the consolation of rest, the wonder of
dreams, and the sleep of death.

*Morpheus, the god of dreams, was said to drop a wreath of poppies on the
sleeper's heavy head. In the dream of the red poppy, the lover seeks erotic
passion. White poppies offer a deeper dream, oceanic and intimate.*

*"Of all flowers, they inspire me," wrote the Chilean poet Pablo Neruda,
of poppies.*

Water Lily

[NYMPHAEA]

The water lily stands for perfect beauty.

The water lily is the first flower mentioned in world literature. In Asia, the flowering water lily, called the lotus, symbolizes absolute truth and purity. The bloom became associated with Buddha himself. The Hindus in India believe that, before its creation as we know it, the world was a golden lotus.

These water plants, with their flowers of pink, white, and blue, often bloom only at night, their perfume spreading across the dark surface of a pond. In the West, the water lily was given the botanical name nymphaea, referring to those Greek nature goddesses, the nymphs.

Daisy

[BELLIS PERENNIS]

Daisies suggest **innocence.**

The name comes from the Old English *dægeseage, day's eye,* so called because of the pupil-like yellow center of this round white flower, and from the habit of daisies to shut their petals when the sun is gone.

The Greeks tell this story of the daisy's origin. One morning the wood nymphs decided to dance on the sunny edge of the forest, where the orchards began. The god of the orchards, spying them at their games, drew near to watch. One nymph in particular stung him with her beauty, and he fell instantly in love and rushed at her. But she and her sisters vanished, taking refuge in the form of daisies, growing there at the edge of the forest.

The daisy, wrote poet Walter de la Mare, "makes a skylark of every heart." Botticelli used the daisy in his paintings to symbolize the innocence of the Baby Jesus.

2

LIST OF FLOWERS

Allium, 20

Amaryllis, 11

Anemone, 46

Anthurium, 92

Aster, 62

Bachelor's Button, 51

Bird-of-Paradise, 78

Buttercup, 19

Camellia, 82

Chrysanthemum, 28

Crocus, 24

Daffodil, 72

Dahlia, 30

Daisy, 104

Delphinium, 44

Dogwood, 37

Forget-me-not, 25

Freesia, 90

Gardenia, 35

Gerbera, 23

Gladiolus, 77

Heather, 57

Heliotrope, 48

Hibiscus, 88

Hollyhock, 65

Honeysuckle, 66

Hyacinth, 64

Hydrangea, 61

Iris, 49

Jasmine, 33

Lavender, 56

Lilac, 58

Lily, 26

Narcissus, 31

Nasturtium, 54

Magnolia, 12

Marigold, 74

Mimosa, 80

Orchid, 17

Pansy, 53

Peony, 14

Periwinkle, 99

Plumeria, 81

Pomegranate, 93

Poppy, 100

Primrose, 75

Protea, 94

Queen Anne's Lace, 98

Quince, 91

Ranunculus, 87

Rose (Red), 41

Rose (White), 42

Rose (Yellow), 38

Rosemary, 21

Snapdragon, 84

Sunflower, 71

Sweet Pea, 18

Tulip, 68

Violet, 97

Water Lily, 103

Wisteria, 43

Zinnia, 63

Acknowledgments

We would like to thank the many people who gave so generously of their time and energy to this book. Special thanks goes to Tricia Tang for her inspiring flowers; Jim Paul, Kathy Evans, and Francis Bowles who all worked wonders with the text; and Elvis Swift for his beautiful calligraphy. Many thanks also to Jane Field, Irving Gershenz, and Randy Hild. Lastly, unending gratitude goes to Leslie Jonath, our editor, who accepted this project almost instantly and guided it passionately and constantly through the process. It was her ongoing patience, enthusiasm, and care that began this book and nurtured it into being.

To create a little flower is the labor of ages.

—WILLIAM BLAKE